Classic

THAI

Classic
THAI

Subtle and aromatic recipes from the East

KIT CHAN

ULTIMATE
E D I T I O N S

First published by Ultimate Editions in 1997

Ultimate Editions is an imprint of
Anness Publishing Limited
Hermes House
88-89 Blackfriars Road
London SE1 8HA

ISBN 1 86035 217 0

Publisher Joanna Lorenz
Senior Cookery Editor Linda Fraser
Project Editor Zoe Antoniou
Designer Annie Moss
Mac Artist John Fowler
Illustrations Madeleine David
Jacket photography Thomas Odulate
Food for photography Kit Chan

Printed and bound in Singapore

For all recipes, quantities are given in both metric and imperial measures, and, where appropriate,
measures are also given in standard cups and spoons. Follow one set, but not a mixture,
because they are not interchangeable.

Picture on frontispiece: Steamed Seafood Packets, Spring Rolls, Pork Satay and Golden Pouches

1 3 5 7 9 10 8 6 4 2

CONTENTS

INTRODUCTION

Thailand is probably one of the most diverse and complex countries in Asia. Geographically, it is halfway between India and China and so it is hardly surprising that the cultures of its neighbours have influenced the development of its national cuisine.

Thailand is divided into five regions that have distinct geographical and cultural differences; from dense jungles and mountainous retreats to vast plains of paddy-fields, untamed rivers to white sandy beaches and the warm clear ocean.

The climate is tropical so there is an abundance of fruit, vegetables and flowers. Indeed, freshly picked vegetables, aromatic herbs and flavourful leaves are essential to Thai cooking. Vegetables may be stir-fried, steamed or boiled.

The carving of fruits and vegetables into exotic sculptures, decorated with flowers and foliage, has become an art form in Thailand. The country also boasts over one thousand varieties of orchids and the orchid has become an emblem for it.

Food is a celebration. To have to eat alone ranks high on the Thai scale of misfortunes. Throughout Thailand, food and snacking are inescapable parts of life, and there is a constant supply of spicy titbits available wherever one goes.

The variety of snacks is huge. Some dishes are small, such as savoury pastries, spring rolls, steamed dumplings and rice balls. Others, such as noodle dishes, are more substantial and can be a meal in themselves. These snacks are not considered real food in Asia, but merely a pleasurable diversion to while away any spare time, a nibble between meals or a treat at the market. Starters as such are not common in a Thai meal as all the dishes are brought to the table at once.

Cooking is a source of pride and wonder. A Thai cook will always strive for a balance of flavour, texture and colour in a dish, creating a complex range of tastes that are both delicate and magical. Presentation varies from simple plastic bowls at pavement stalls to beautifully decorated china and artistic displays in the finer restaurants.

A Thai meal offers a combination of flavours: sweet, hot, sour, salty and sometimes bitter. Thailand offers a tropical cornucopia of good things to eat and the coastal region yields an abundance of seafood, both tempting and exotic. Usually, in addition to the obligatory bowl of rice, there will be a variety of dishes including a soup, a curry, a steamed dish, a fried one, a salad and one or two sauces. This makes eating a Thai meal particularly enjoyable and special.

Opposite (clockwise from top): three classic rice and noodle dishes; Fried Jasmine Rice, Phat Thai and Special Chow Mein

Above (clockwise from top): lemon grass, Thai shallots, kaffir limes and fresh kaffir lime leaves

There should be no duplication or repetition, and ingredients and colours should be as diverse as possible. This reflects the influence of the Chinese principle of yin and yang; the idea is to achieve overall healthful harmony by balancing opposing qualities. The portion size will depend on the number of people eating. All the dishes are placed on the table at the same time and shared. They are not eaten in any particular order.

Water and tea are the most common drinks served with a meal. Thai whisky is often drunk at festive gatherings. But soup is also a very significant part of a Thai's daily fare. It can be served as a snack or a light lunch. A bowl of soup is nearly always included in a Thai meal. It is placed on the table alongside the other dishes, to be enjoyed a little at a time, as a liquid refreshment as and when each diner chooses.

Equipment (right, clockwise from top): two-tier bamboo steamer, large granite pestle and mortar, wooden chopping board with cleaver, large cook's knife and small paring knife, wire-basket draining spoon and wok.

Thai soups, which are quick and easy to prepare, are usually based on a light broth and many are enriched with coconut milk or cream, like the Pumpkin and Coconut Soup.

Without doubt the most famous soup is *Tom Yam Goong* – Hot and Sour Prawn Soup with Lemon Grass, a symphony of flavour, using many local favourites such as galangal,

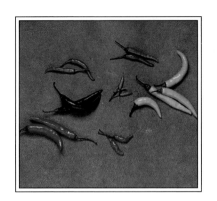

Clockwise from top: green chillies, Thai orange chillies, Indian chillies, red chillies, and mild green chillies

coriander, kaffir lime leaves and chillies.

Indeed, the most prevalent flavour in Thai cooking comes from the chilli, which surprisingly was introduced to the country during the sixteenth century by Portuguese missionaries. It didn't take the Thais long to make good use of it, believing that chillies cool the body, stimulate the appetite and bring balance and harmony to their food.

Curries are also a prominent part of a selection of dishes in a main meal. All curry-making begins with the curry paste. In days gone by, each household would have its own recipes, handed down from generation to generation. Various herbs and spices are used, and are crushed with a pestle and mortar, resulting in an aromatic and fragrant wet paste, which can range from mild to extremely hot. The hottest are the green curry pastes.

Curries originated from southern India, but unlike Indian curries that use a lot of dried powdered spices and are thick and simmer for many hours, Thai curries are fresher and much lighter. They are usually thin and soup-like and require a lot less cooking, with the exception of the dish known as Mussaman curry.

In former times, Thais were accustomed to eating with their fingers, pressing rice into small balls, which were dipped into dishes. Today, they eat with a large spoon to scoop up sauces and a fork to mix and push food on to the spoon. Knives are rarely used because meat is usually served in small pieces, and chopsticks are used only to eat Chinese-style noodles.

Thais tend to cook by "feel", taking into account the tastes and preferences of their family. You should always taste and adjust the seasoning as you like it. If you find something is too salty or too sweet and, even more importantly, if you are not used to the hotness of chillies, add a little at a time until you get a balance that you like. In short, Thai cuisine is light and fresh, with delicately balanced spices and a harmony of flavours, colours and textures designed to appeal to both the eyes and the palate. It may take some time for a novice to grasp the idea of preparing so many dishes, but the rewards are great, for there is something to appeal to everyone.

STEAMED SEAFOOD PACKETS

Very neat and delicate, these steamed packets make an excellent starter or a light lunch. You can find banana leaves in oriental or Caribbean supermarkets.

INGREDIENTS
225g/8oz crab meat
50g/2oz shelled prawns, chopped
6 water chestnuts, chopped
30ml/2 tbsp chopped bamboo shoots
15ml/1 tbsp chopped spring onion
5ml/1 tsp chopped root ginger
15ml/1 tbsp soy sauce
15ml/1 tbsp fish sauce
12 rice sheets
banana leaves
oil, for brushing
2 spring onions, shredded,
2 red chillies, seeded and sliced,
and coriander leaves, to garnish

SERVES 4

1 Combine the crab meat, chopped prawns, water chestnuts, bamboo shoots, chopped spring onion and ginger in a bowl. Mix well, then add the soy sauce and fish sauce. Stir until blended.

2 Take a rice sheet and dip it in warm water. Place it on a flat surface and leave for a few seconds to soften.

3 Place a spoonful of the filling in the centre of the sheet and fold into a square packet. Repeat with the rest of the rice sheets and seafood mixture.

4 Use banana leaves to line a steamer, then brush them with oil. Place the packets, seam-side down, on the leaves and steam over a high heat for 6–8 minutes or until the filling is cooked.

5 Transfer on to a plate and serve, garnished with the shredded spring onions, sliced chillies and coriander.

COOK'S TIP
The seafood packets will spread out when steamed, so be sure to space them well apart to prevent them sticking together.

GOLDEN POUCHES

These crisp pouches are delicious served as an appetizer or to accompany drinks at a party.

INGREDIENTS
115g/4oz minced pork
115g/4oz crab meat
2–3 wood ears, soaked and chopped
15ml/1 tbsp chopped coriander
5ml/1 tsp chopped garlic
30ml/2 tbsp chopped spring onions
1 egg
15ml/1 tbsp fish sauce
5ml/1 tsp soy sauce
pinch of granulated sugar
20 wonton wrappers
20 long chives, blanched (optional)
oil, for deep frying
freshly ground black pepper
plum or sweet chilli sauce, to serve

MAKES ABOUT 20

1 In a mixing bowl, combine the pork, crab meat, wood ears, coriander, garlic, spring onions and egg. Mix well and season with fish sauce, soy sauce, sugar and freshly ground black pepper.

2 Take a wonton wrapper and place it on a flat surface. Put a heaped teaspoonful of filling in the centre of the wrapper, then pull up the edges of the pastry around the filling.

3 Pinch together to seal. If you like, you can go a step further and tie it with a long chive. Repeat with the remaining pork mixture and wonton wrappers.

4 Heat the oil in a wok or deep-fat fryer. Fry the wontons in batches until they are crisp and golden brown. Drain on kitchen paper and serve immediately with either a plum or sweet chilli sauce.

PORK SATAY

Originating in Indonesia, satay are skewers of meat marinated with spices and grilled quickly over charcoal. You can make them with chicken, beef or lamb.

INGREDIENTS
450g/1lb lean pork
5ml/1 tsp grated root ginger
1 lemon grass stalk, finely chopped
3 garlic cloves, finely chopped
15ml/1 tbsp medium curry paste
5ml/1 tsp ground cumin
5ml/1 tsp ground turmeric
60ml/4 tbsp coconut cream
30ml/2 tbsp fish sauce
5ml/1 tsp granulated sugar
20 wooden satay skewers
oil, for brushing
sprigs of mint, to garnish

FOR THE SATAY SAUCE
250ml/8fl oz/1 cup coconut milk
30ml/2 tbsp red curry paste
75g/3oz crunchy peanut butter
120ml/4fl oz/½ cup chicken stock
45ml/3 tbsp brown sugar
30ml/2 tbsp tamarind juice
15ml/1 tbsp fish sauce
2.5ml/½ tsp salt

MAKES ABOUT 20

1 Cut the pork thinly into 5cm/2in strips. Mix together the ginger, lemon grass, garlic, medium curry paste, cumin, turmeric, coconut cream, fish sauce and sugar.

2 Pour over the pork and leave to marinate for about 2 hours.

3 Meanwhile, make the sauce. Heat the coconut milk over a medium heat, then add the red curry paste, peanut butter, chicken stock and sugar.

4 Cook and stir until smooth, for about 5–6 minutes. Add the tamarind juice, fish sauce and salt to taste.

5 Thread the meat on to skewers. Brush with oil and grill over charcoal or under a preheated grill for 3–4 minutes on each side, turning occasionally, until cooked. Garnish with mint and serve with the satay sauce.

SPRING ROLLS

These crunchy spring rolls are as popular in Thai cuisine as they are in Chinese. Thais fill their version with a garlic, pork and noodle filling. Serve the rolls with Thai sweet chilli sauce for dipping, if you wish.

INGREDIENTS
4–6 dried Chinese mushrooms, soaked
50g/2oz bean thread noodles, soaked
vegetable oil, for frying
2 garlic cloves, chopped
2 red chillies, seeded and chopped
225g/8oz minced pork
50g/2oz chopped cooked prawns
30ml/2 tbsp fish sauce
5ml/1 tsp granulated sugar
1 carrot, finely shredded
50g/2oz bamboo shoots, chopped
50g/2oz beansprouts
2 spring onions, chopped
15ml/1 tbsp chopped coriander
30ml/2 tbsp flour
24 × 15cm/6in square
spring roll wrappers
freshly ground black pepper

MAKES ABOUT 24

1 Drain and chop the mushrooms. Drain the noodles and cut into 5cm/2in lengths.

2 Heat 30ml/2 tbsp oil in a wok or frying pan, add the garlic and chillies and fry for 30 seconds. Add the pork, stirring until the meat is browned.

3 Add the noodles, mushrooms and prawns. Season with fish sauce, sugar and pepper. Tip into a bowl.

4 Mix in the carrot, bamboo shoots, beansprouts, spring onions and chopped coriander for the filling. Reserve a little to use as a garnish.

5 In a bowl, mix the flour to a paste with a little water. Place a spoonful of filling in the centre of a spring roll wrapper.

6 Turn the bottom edge over to cover the filling, then fold in the left and right sides. Roll up almost to the top edge. Brush the top edge with flour paste and seal. Repeat with the rest of the wrappers.

7 Heat some oil in a wok or deep-fat fryer. Slide in the spring rolls a few at a time and fry until crisp and golden brown. Remove with a slotted spoon and drain on kitchen paper. Serve hot, garnished with the reserved vegetables.

PAN-STEAMED MUSSELS WITH THAI HERBS

nother simple dish to prepare. The lemon grass adds a refreshing tang to the mussels.

INGREDIENTS
1kg/2¼lb mussels, cleaned and
beards removed
2 lemon grass stalks, finely chopped
4 shallots, chopped
4 kaffir lime leaves, roughly torn
2 red chillies, seeded and sliced
15ml/1 tbsp fish sauce
30ml/2 tbsp lime juice
2 spring onions, chopped, and
coriander leaves, to garnish

SERVES 4–6

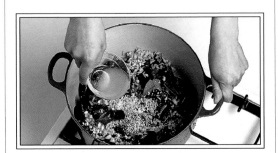

1 Place all the ingredients, except for the spring onions and coriander, in a large saucepan and stir thoroughly.

2 Cover and steam for 5–7 minutes, shaking the saucepan occasionally, until the mussels open. Discard any mussels that do not open.

3 Transfer the cooked mussels to a warmed serving dish.

4 Garnish the mussels with chopped spring onions and coriander leaves. Serve immediately.

FISH CAKES WITH CUCUMBER RELISH

These wonderful small fish cakes are a familiar and popular appetizer, usually accompanied by Thai beer.

INGREDIENTS
300g/11oz white fish fillet, such as cod,
cut into chunks
30ml/2 tbsp red curry paste
1 egg
30ml/2 tbsp fish sauce
5ml/1 tsp granulated sugar
30ml/2 tbsp cornflour
3 kaffir lime leaves, shredded
15ml/1 tbsp chopped coriander
50g/2oz green beans, finely sliced
oil, for frying
Chinese mustard cress, to garnish

FOR THE CUCUMBER RELISH
60ml/4 tbsp Thai coconut
or rice vinegar
60ml/4 tbsp water
50g/2oz sugar
1 head of pickled garlic
1 cucumber, quartered and sliced
4 shallots, finely sliced
15ml/1 tbsp finely chopped root ginger
2 red chillies, seeded and finely sliced

MAKES ABOUT 12

1 To make the cucumber relish, bring the vinegar, water and sugar to the boil. Stir until the sugar dissolves, then remove from the heat and cool.

2 Combine the rest of the relish ingredients together in a bowl and pour over the vinegar mixture.

3 Combine the fish, curry paste and egg in a food processor and process well. Transfer the mixture to a bowl, add the rest of the ingredients, except for the oil and garnish, and mix well.

4 Mould and shape the mixture into cakes about 5cm/2in in diameter and 5mm/¼in thick.

5 Heat the oil in a wok or deep-fat fryer. Fry the fish cakes, a few at a time, for about 4–5 minutes or until golden brown. Remove and drain on kitchen paper. Garnish with Chinese mustard cress and serve with the cucumber relish.

CHIANG MAI NOODLE SOUP

A signature dish of the city of Chiang Mai, this delicious noodle soup has Burmese origins and is the Thai equivalent of the Malaysian "Laksa".

INGREDIENTS

600ml/1 pint/2½ cups coconut milk
30ml/2 tbsp red curry paste
5ml/1 tsp ground turmeric
450g/1lb chicken thighs, boned and cut into bite-size chunks
600ml/1 pint/2½ cups chicken stock
60ml/4 tbsp fish sauce
15ml/1 tbsp dark soy sauce
juice of ½–1 lime
450g/1lb fresh egg noodles, blanched briefly in boiling water
salt and freshly ground black pepper

FOR THE GARNISH

3 spring onions, chopped
4 red chillies, seeded and chopped
4 shallots, chopped
60ml/4 tbsp sliced pickled mustard leaves, rinsed
30ml/2 tbsp fried sliced garlic coriander leaves
4 fried noodle nests (optional)

SERVES 4–6

1 Put one third of the coconut milk into a large saucepan, bring to the boil and stir with a wooden spoon until it separates.

2 Add the curry paste and ground turmeric, stir to mix completely and cook until fragrant.

3 Add the chicken and stir-fry for about 2 minutes, ensuring that all the chunks are coated with the paste.

4 Add the remaining coconut milk, chicken stock, fish sauce and soy sauce. Season with salt and freshly ground black pepper to taste. Simmer gently for about 7–10 minutes. Remove from the heat and stir in the lime juice.

5 Reheat the noodles in boiling water, drain and divide between individual bowls. Divide the chicken between the bowls and ladle in the hot soup. Top each serving with a few of each of the garnishes.

HOT AND SOUR PRAWN SOUP WITH LEMON GRASS

This is a classic seafood soup – *Tom Yam Goong* – and is probably the most popular of Thai soups.

INGREDIENTS

450g/1lb king prawns (raw or cooked)
1 litre/1¾ pints/4 cups chicken stock or water
3 lemon grass stalks
10 kaffir lime leaves, torn in half
225g/8oz can straw mushrooms, drained
45ml/3 tbsp fish sauce
50ml/2fl oz/¼ cup lime juice
30ml/2 tbsp chopped spring onions
15ml/1 tbsp coriander leaves
4 red chillies, seeded and chopped

SERVES 4–6

1 Shell and devein the prawns and set aside. Rinse the prawn shells, place in a large saucepan with the stock or water and bring to the boil.

2 Bruise the lemon grass stalks with the blunt edge of a chopping knife and add them to the stock together with half of the lime leaves. Simmer gently for 5–6 minutes, until the stalks change colour and the stock is fragrant.

3 Strain the stock, return to the saucepan and reheat. Add the mushrooms and prawns, then cook for a few minutes, or until the prawns turn pink if raw.

4 Stir in the fish sauce, lime juice, spring onions, coriander, chillies and the rest of the lime leaves. Taste; adjust the flavours. It should be sour, salty, spicy and hot.

SPINACH AND BEAN CURD SOUP

An extremely delicate and mild-flavoured soup that can be used to counterbalance the heat from a hot Thai curry.

INGREDIENTS

30ml/2 tbsp dried shrimps
1 litre/1¾ pints/4 cups chicken stock
225g/8oz fresh bean curd, drained and cut into 2cm/¾in cubes
30ml/2 tbsp fish sauce
350g/12oz fresh spinach leaves, thoroughly washed
freshly ground black pepper
2 spring onions, finely sliced, to garnish

SERVES 4–6

3 Tear the spinach leaves into bite-size pieces and add to the soup. Cook for another 1–2 minutes.

4 Remove the soup from the heat, ladle into bowls and sprinkle over the finely sliced spring onions, to garnish.

1 Rinse and drain the dried shrimps. Combine the shrimps with the chicken stock in a saucepan and bring to the boil.

2 Add the bean curd and simmer for about 5 minutes. Season with fish sauce and black pepper to taste.

PUMPKIN AND COCONUT SOUP

Enriched with smooth coconut cream, this is another soup which thrills the taste buds with a combination of exotic flavours.

INGREDIENTS

2 garlic cloves, crushed

4 shallots, finely chopped

2.5ml/½ tsp shrimp paste

15ml/1 tbsp dried shrimps soaked for 10 minutes and drained

1 lemon grass stalk, chopped

2 green chillies, seeded

600ml/1 pint/2½ cups chicken stock

450g/1lb pumpkin, cut into 2cm/¾in thick chunks

600ml/1 pint/2½ cups coconut cream

30ml/2 tbsp fish sauce

5ml/1 tsp granulated sugar

115g/4oz small cooked shelled prawns

salt and freshly ground black pepper

2 red chillies, seeded and finely sliced, and 10–12 basil leaves, to garnish

SERVES 4–6

1 Grind the garlic, shallots, shrimp paste, dried shrimps, lemon grass, green chillies and salt to taste into a paste.

2 In a large saucepan, bring the chicken stock to the boil, add the ground paste and stir to dissolve.

COOK'S TIP

Shrimp paste, which is made from ground shrimps fermented in brine, is used to give food a savoury flavour.

3 Add the pumpkin chunks and simmer gently for about 10–15 minutes or until the pumpkin is tender.

4 Stir in the coconut cream, then bring back to a simmer. Add the fish sauce, sugar and ground black pepper to taste.

5 Add the prawns and cook until they are heated through. Serve garnished with the sliced red chillies and basil leaves.

MIXED VEGETABLES IN COCONUT MILK

A most delicious way of cooking vegetables. If you don't like highly spiced food, use fewer red chillies.

INGREDIENTS
450g/1lb mixed vegetables, such as
aubergines, baby sweetcorn, carrots,
snake beans and patty pan squash
8 red chillies, seeded
2 lemon grass stalks, chopped
4 kaffir lime leaves, torn
30ml/2 tbsp vegetable oil
250ml/8fl oz/1 cup coconut milk
30ml/2 tbsp fish sauce
salt
15–20 Thai basil leaves, to garnish

SERVES 4–6

2 Put the red chillies, lemon grass and kaffir lime leaves in a mortar and grind together with a pestle.

3 Heat the oil in a wok or large deep frying pan. Add the chilli mixture and fry for 2–3 minutes.

4 Stir in the coconut milk and bring to the boil. Add the vegetables and cook for about 5 minutes or until they are tender. Season with the fish sauce and salt, and garnish with Thai basil leaves.

1 Cut the vegetables into similar-size shapes using a sharp knife.

BAMBOO SHOOT SALAD

This salad, which has a hot and sharp flavour, originated in north-east Thailand. Use fresh, young bamboo shoots when you can find them, otherwise substitute canned bamboo shoots.

INGREDIENTS
400g/14oz can whole bamboo shoots
25g/1oz glutinous rice
30ml/2 tbsp chopped shallots
15ml/1 tbsp chopped garlic
45ml/3 tbsp chopped spring onions
30ml/2 tbsp fish sauce
30ml/2 tbsp lime juice
5ml/1 tsp granulated sugar
2.5ml/½ tsp dried flaked chillies
20–25 small mint leaves
15ml/1 tbsp toasted sesame seeds

SERVES 4

1 Rinse and drain the bamboo shoots, finely slice and set aside.

2 Dry-roast the rice in a frying pan until it is golden brown. Remove and grind to fine crumbs with a pestle and mortar.

3 Tip the rice into a bowl, add the shallots, garlic, spring onions, fish sauce, lime juice, granulated sugar, chillies and half the mint leaves.

4 Mix thoroughly, then pour over the bamboo shoots and toss together. Serve sprinkled with sesame seeds and the remaining mint leaves.

LARP OF CHIANG MAI

Chiang Mai is a city in the north-east of Thailand. The city is culturally very close to Laos and famous for its chicken salad, which was originally called "Laap" or "Larp". Duck, beef or pork can be used instead of chicken.

INGREDIENTS
450g/1lb minced chicken
1 lemon grass stalk, finely chopped
3 kaffir lime leaves, finely chopped
4 red chillies, seeded and chopped
60ml/4 tbsp lime juice
30ml/2 tbsp fish sauce
15ml/1 tbsp roasted ground rice
2 spring onions, chopped
30ml/2 tbsp coriander leaves
mixed salad leaves, to serve
cucumber and tomato slices, and a few sprigs of mint, to garnish

SERVES 4–6

1 Heat a large non-stick frying pan. Add the minced chicken and a little water to moisten while cooking.

2 Stir constantly until cooked; this will take about 7–10 minutes.

3 Transfer the cooked chicken to a large bowl and add the rest of the ingredients. Mix thoroughly.

4 Serve on a bed of mixed salad leaves and garnish with cucumber, tomato slices and a few sprigs of mint.

COOK'S TIP
Use sticky, or glutinous, rice to make roasted ground rice. Put the rice in a frying pan and dry-roast until golden brown. Remove and grind to a powder in a pestle and mortar or in a food processor. Keep in a glass jar in a cool and dry place and use as required.

CABBAGE SALAD

A simple and delicious way of using cabbage. Other vegetables such as broccoli, calabrese, cauliflower and Chinese cabbage can also be used.

INGREDIENTS

30ml/2 tbsp fish sauce
grated rind of 1 lime
30ml/2 tbsp lime juice
120ml/4fl oz/½ cup coconut milk
30ml/2 tbsp vegetable oil
2 large red chillies, seeded and
cut into fine strips
6 garlic cloves, finely sliced
6 shallots, finely sliced
1 small cabbage, shredded
30ml/2 tbsp coarsely chopped roasted
peanuts, to serve

SERVES 4–6

1 Make the dressing by combining the fish sauce, lime rind and juice and coconut milk. Set aside.

2 Heat the oil in a wok or frying pan. Stir-fry the chillies, garlic and shallots, until the shallots are brown and crisp. Remove and set aside.

3 Blanch the cabbage in boiling salted water for about 2–3 minutes, drain and put into a bowl.

4 Stir the dressing into the cabbage, toss and mix well. Transfer the salad into a serving dish. Sprinkle with the fried shallot mixture and the chopped roasted peanuts.

THAI BEEF SALAD

A hearty salad of beef, laced with a chilli and lime dressing that perfectly complements the meat.

INGREDIENTS
2 × 225g/8oz sirloin steaks
1 red onion, finely sliced
½ cucumber, cut into thin ribbons
1 lemon grass stalk, finely chopped
30ml/2 tbsp chopped spring onions
juice of 2 limes
15–30ml/1–2 tbsp fish sauce
2–4 red chillies, finely sliced, fresh coriander, Chinese mustard cress and mint leaves, to garnish

SERVES 4

1 Pan-fry or grill the sirloin steaks to medium-rare. Set aside to rest for about 10–15 minutes.

2 When cool, thinly slice the beef and put the slices in a large bowl.

3 Add the sliced onion, cucumber ribbons and lemon grass.

4 Add the spring onions. Toss and season with lime juice and fish sauce. Serve at room temperature or chilled, garnished with the sliced chillies, coriander, Chinese mustard cress and mint leaves.

TANGY CHICKEN SALAD

This fresh and lively dish typifies the character of Thai cuisine. It is ideal for a starter or light lunch.

INGREDIENTS
4 skinned, boneless chicken breasts
2 garlic cloves, crushed and roughly chopped
30ml/2 tbsp soy sauce
30ml/2 tbsp vegetable oil
120ml/4fl oz/½ cup coconut cream
30ml/2 tbsp fish sauce
juice of 1 lime
30ml/2 tbsp palm sugar
115g/4oz water chestnuts, sliced
50g/2oz cashew nuts, roasted
4 shallots, finely sliced
4 kaffir lime leaves, finely sliced
1 lemon grass stalk, finely sliced
5ml/1 tsp chopped galangal
1 large red chilli, seeded and finely sliced
2 spring onions, finely sliced
10–12 mint leaves, torn
1 head of lettuce, to serve
sprigs of coriander and 2 red chillies, seeded and sliced, to garnish

SERVES 4–6

1 Trim the chicken breasts of any excess fat and put them in a large dish. Rub with the garlic, soy sauce and 15ml/1 tbsp of the oil. Leave to marinate for 1–2 hours.

2 Grill or pan-fry the chicken for 3–4 minutes on both sides or until cooked. Remove and set aside to cool.

3 In a small saucepan, heat the coconut cream, fish sauce, lime juice and palm sugar. Stir until all of the sugar has dissolved and then remove from the heat.

4 Cut the cooked chicken into strips and combine with the water chestnuts, cashew nuts, shallots, kaffir lime leaves, lemon grass, galangal, red chilli, spring onions and mint leaves.

5 Pour the coconut dressing over the chicken, toss and mix well. Serve the chicken on a bed of lettuce leaves and garnish with sprigs of coriander and sliced red chillies.

BAKED FISH IN BANANA LEAVES

F ish that is prepared in this way is particularly succulent and flavourful. Fillets are used here rather than whole fish – easier for those who don't like to mess about with bones. It is a great dish for outdoor barbecues.

INGREDIENTS
250ml/8fl oz/1 cup coconut milk
30ml/2 tbsp red curry paste
45ml/3 tbsp fish sauce
30ml/2 tbsp caster sugar
5 kaffir lime leaves, torn
4 × 175g/6oz fish fillets, such
as snapper
175g/6oz mixed vegetables, such as
carrots or leeks, finely shredded
4 banana leaves
30ml/2 tbsp shredded spring onions,
and 2 red chillies, finely sliced,
to garnish

SERVES 4

1 Combine the coconut milk, curry paste, fish sauce, sugar and kaffir lime leaves in a shallow dish.

2 Marinate the fish in this mixture for about 15–30 minutes. Preheat the oven to 200°C/400°F/Gas 6.

3 Mix the vegetables together and lay a portion on top of a banana leaf. Place a piece of fish on top, together with a little of its marinade.

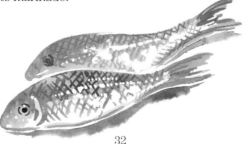

4 Wrap the fish up by turning in the sides and ends of the leaf and secure with cocktail sticks. Repeat with the rest of the leaves and fish.

5 Bake in the hot oven for 20–25 minutes or until the fish is cooked. Alternatively, cook under the grill or on the barbecue. Just before serving, garnish with a sprinkling of spring onions and sliced red chillies.

STIR-FRIED SCALLOPS WITH ASPARAGUS

Asparagus is extremely popular among the Chinese Thai. The combination of garlic and black pepper gives this dish its spiciness. You can replace the scallops with prawns or other firm fish.

INGREDIENTS

60ml/4 tbsp vegetable oil
1 bunch asparagus, cut into
5cm/2in lengths
4 garlic cloves, finely chopped
2 shallots, finely chopped
450g/1lb scallops, cleaned
30ml/2 tbsp fish sauce
2.5ml/½ tsp coarsely ground
black pepper
120ml/4fl oz/½ cup coconut milk
coriander leaves, to garnish

SERVES 4–6

1 Heat half the oil in a wok or large frying pan. Add the asparagus and stir-fry for about 2 minutes. Transfer the asparagus to a plate and set aside.

2 Add the rest of the oil, garlic and shallots to the same wok and fry until fragrant. Add the scallops, stir and cook for another 1–2 minutes.

3 Return the asparagus to the wok. Add the fish sauce, ground black pepper and coconut milk.

4 Stir and cook for another 3–4 minutes or until the scallops and asparagus are cooked. Garnish with the coriander leaves.

SATAY PRAWNS

n enticing and tasty dish. Lightly cooked greens and jasmine rice make good accompaniments.

INGREDIENTS
*450g/1lb king prawns, shelled, tail ends
left intact and deveined
½ bunch coriander leaves, 4 red chillies,
finely sliced, and spring onions, cut
diagonally, to garnish*

FOR THE PEANUT SAUCE
*45ml/3 tbsp vegetable oil
15ml/1 tbsp chopped garlic
1 small onion, chopped
3–4 red chillies, crushed and chopped
3 kaffir lime leaves, torn
1 lemon grass stalk, bruised
and chopped
5ml/1 tsp medium curry paste
250ml/8fl oz/1 cup coconut milk
1.5cm/½in cinnamon stick
75g/3oz crunchy peanut butter
45ml/3 tbsp tamarind juice
30ml/2 tbsp fish sauce
30ml/2 tbsp palm sugar
juice of ½ lemon*

SERVES 4–6

1 To make the sauce, heat half the oil in a wok or large frying pan and add the garlic and onion. Cook until it softens, about 3–4 minutes.

2 Add the chillies, kaffir lime leaves, lemon grass and curry paste. Cook for a further 2–3 minutes.

3 Stir in the coconut milk, cinnamon stick, peanut butter, tamarind juice, fish sauce, palm sugar and lemon juice.

4 Reduce the heat and simmer gently for 15–20 minutes until the sauce thickens, stirring occasionally to ensure the sauce doesn't stick to the bottom of the wok or frying pan.

5 Heat the rest of the oil in a wok or large frying pan. Add the prawns and stir-fry for about 3–4 minutes or until the prawns turn pink and are slightly firm to the touch.

6 Mix the prawns with the sauce. Serve garnished with coriander leaves, red chillies and spring onions.

SWEET AND SOUR PORK, THAI-STYLE

S weet and sour is traditionally a Chinese creation but the Thais also do it very well. This version has an altogether fresher and cleaner flavour and it makes a good one-dish meal when served over rice.

INGREDIENTS
350g/12oz lean pork
30ml/2 tbsp vegetable oil
4 garlic cloves, finely sliced
1 small red onion, sliced
30ml/2 tbsp fish sauce
15ml/1 tbsp granulated sugar
1 red pepper, seeded and diced
½ cucumber, seeded and sliced
2 plum tomatoes, cut into wedges
115g/4oz pineapple, cut into small chunks
2 spring onions, cut into short lengths
freshly ground black pepper
coriander leaves and spring onions, shredded, to garnish

SERVES 4

1 Slice the pork into thin strips. Heat the oil in a wok or large frying pan.

2 Add the garlic and fry until golden, then add the pork and stir-fry for about 4–5 minutes. Add the onion.

3 Season with fish sauce, sugar and freshly ground black pepper. Stir and cook for 3–4 minutes, or until the pork is cooked.

4 Add the rest of the vegetables, the pineapple and spring onions. You may need to add a few tablespoons of water. Continue to stir-fry for another 3–4 minutes. Serve hot, garnished with coriander leaves and spring onions.

BARBECUED CHICKEN

Barbecued chicken is served almost everywhere in Thailand, from portable roadside stalls to sports stadiums and beaches. For an authentic touch, serve with rice on a banana leaf.

INGREDIENTS
1 chicken, about 1.5kg/3–3½ lb,
cut into 8–10 pieces
2 limes, cut into wedges,
2 red chillies, finely sliced, and
a few lemon grass stalks, to garnish

FOR THE MARINADE
2 lemon grass stalks, chopped
2.5cm/1in piece fresh root ginger
6 garlic cloves
4 shallots
½ bunch coriander roots
15ml/1 tbsp palm sugar
120ml/4fl oz/½ cup coconut milk
30ml/2 tbsp fish sauce
30ml/2 tbsp soy sauce

SERVES 4–6

1 To make the marinade, put all the ingredients into a food processor and process until smooth.

2 Put the chicken pieces in a dish and pour over the marinade. Leave in a cool place to marinate for at least 4 hours, or preferably overnight.

3 Barbecue the chicken over glowing coals, or place it on a rack over a baking tray and bake at 200°C/400°F/Gas 6 for about 20–30 minutes or until the chicken is cooked and golden brown. Turn the pieces occasionally and brush with the marinade.

4 Garnish with lime wedges, finely sliced red chillies and lemon grass.

STIR-FRIED CHICKEN WITH BASIL AND CHILLIES

This quick and easy chicken dish is an excellent introduction to Thai cuisine. Deep frying the basil adds another dimension to this recipe. Thai basil, also known as holy basil, has a unique, pungent flavour that is both spicy and sharp. The dull leaves have serrated edges.

INGREDIENTS
45ml/3 tbsp vegetable oil
4 garlic cloves, sliced
2–4 red chillies, seeded and chopped
450g/1lb chicken, cut into bite-size pieces
30–45ml/2–3 tbsp fish sauce
10ml/2 tsp dark soy sauce
5ml/1 tsp sugar
10–12 Thai basil leaves
2 red chillies, finely sliced, and 20 Thai basil leaves, deep fried (optional), to garnish

SERVES 4–6

COOK'S TIP
To deep fry Thai basil leaves, make sure that the leaves are completely dry. Deep fry in hot oil for about 30–40 seconds, lift out and drain on kitchen paper.

1 Heat the oil in a wok or large frying pan and swirl it around.

2 Add the garlic and chillies and stir-fry until golden.

3 Add the chicken and stir-fry until it changes colour.

4 Season with fish sauce, soy sauce and sugar. Continue to stir-fry for another 3–4 minutes or until the chicken is cooked through. Stir in the fresh Thai basil leaves. Garnish with sliced red chillies and the deep fried basil, if using.

FRAGRANT THAI MEATBALLS

A creamy peanut sauce accompanies these tasty little meatballs, which can be made of pork or beef.

INGREDIENTS
450g/1lb lean minced pork or beef
15ml/1 tbsp chopped garlic
1 lemon grass stalk, finely chopped
4 spring onions, finely chopped
15ml/1 tbsp chopped fresh coriander
30ml/2 tbsp red curry paste
15ml/1 tbsp lemon juice
15ml/1 tbsp fish sauce
1 egg
salt and freshly ground black pepper
rice flour, for dusting
oil, for deep frying
sprigs of coriander, to garnish

FOR THE PEANUT SAUCE
15ml/1 tbsp vegetable oil
15ml/1 tbsp red curry paste
30ml/2 tbsp crunchy peanut butter
15ml/1 tbsp palm sugar
15ml/1 tbsp lemon juice
250ml/8fl oz/1 cup coconut milk

SERVES 4–6

1 Make the peanut sauce. Heat the oil in a small saucepan, add the curry paste and fry for 1 minute.

2 Stir in the rest of the sauce ingredients and bring to the boil. Lower the heat and simmer for 5 minutes, until the sauce has thickened.

3 Make the meatballs. Combine all the ingredients except for the rice flour, oil and coriander, and add some seasoning. Mix and blend everything together well.

4 Roll and shape the meat into small balls about the size of a walnut. Dust the meatballs with rice flour.

5 Heat the oil in a wok until hot and deep fry the meatballs in batches until nicely browned and cooked through. Drain on kitchen paper. Serve garnished with sprigs of coriander and accompanied by the peanut sauce.

STIR-FRIED BEEF IN OYSTER SAUCE

Another simple but delicious recipe. In Thailand fresh straw mushrooms are readily available, but oyster mushrooms make a good substitute. To make the dish even more interesting, use several types of mushroom.

INGREDIENTS
450g/1lb rump steak
30ml/2 tbsp soy sauce
15ml/1 tbsp cornflour
45ml/3 tbsp vegetable oil
15ml/1 tbsp chopped garlic
15ml/1 tbsp chopped root ginger
225g/8oz mixed mushrooms, such as
shiitake, oyster and straw
30ml/2 tbsp oyster sauce
5ml/1 tsp granulated sugar
4 spring onions, cut into short lengths
freshly ground black pepper
2 red chillies, cut into strips, to garnish

SERVES 4–6

COOK'S TIP
Made from extracts of oysters, oyster sauce is velvety smooth and has a savoury-sweet and meaty taste. There are several types available; buy the best you can afford.

1 Slice the beef, on the diagonal, into long thin strips. Mix together the soy sauce and cornflour in a large bowl, stir in the beef and leave to marinate for 1–2 hours.

2 Heat half the oil in a wok or frying pan. Add the garlic and ginger and fry until fragrant. Stir in the strips of beef. Stir to separate the pieces, allow them to colour and cook for 1–2 minutes. Remove from the pan and set aside.

3 Heat the remaining oil in the wok. Add your selection of mushrooms, and cook until tender.

4 Return the beef to the wok with the mushrooms. Add the oyster sauce, sugar and freshly ground black pepper to taste. Mix well.

5 Add the spring onions. Mix together. Serve garnished with strips of red chilli.

MUSSAMAN CURRY

This curry is Indian in origin. Traditionally it is made with beef, but chicken or lamb can be used, or you can make a vegetarian version using bean curd. It has a rich, sweet and spicy flavour. Serve with boiled rice.

INGREDIENTS
600ml/1 pint/2½ cups coconut milk
675g/1½lb stewing steak, cut into
2.5cm/1in chunks
250ml/8fl oz/1 cup coconut cream
45ml/3 tbsp Mussaman curry paste
(see Cook's Tip)
30ml/2 tbsp fish sauce
15ml/1 tbsp palm sugar
60ml/4 tbsp tamarind juice
6 cardamom pods
1 cinnamon stick
225g/8oz potatoes, cut into
even-size chunks
1 onion, cut into wedges
50g/2oz roasted peanuts
boiled rice, to serve

SERVES 4–6

1 Bring the coconut milk to a gentle boil in a large saucepan. Add the beef and simmer for about 40 minutes, until tender.

2 Put the coconut cream into a saucepan, then cook for about 5–8 minutes, stirring constantly, until it separates.

3 Add the Mussaman curry paste and fry until fragrant. Add the fried curry paste to the pan containing the cooked beef.

4 Add the fish sauce, sugar, tamarind juice, cardamom pods, cinnamon stick, potato chunks and onion. Simmer until the potatoes are cooked, for 10–15 minutes.

5 Add the roasted peanuts. Cook for a further 5 minutes, then serve with rice.

COOK'S TIP
Mussaman curry paste is used to make the Thai version of a Muslim curry. It can be prepared and then stored in a glass jar in the fridge for up to four months.
Remove the seeds from 12 large dried chillies and soak in hot water for 15 minutes. Combine 60ml/4 tbsp chopped shallots, 5 garlic cloves, 1 chopped lemon grass stalk, 10ml/2 tsp chopped galangal, 5ml/1 tsp cumin seeds, 15ml/1 tbsp coriander seeds, 2 cloves and 6 black peppercorns. Place in a wok and dry-fry over a low heat for 5–6 minutes. Grind or process into a powder and stir in 5ml/1 tsp shrimp paste, 5ml/1 tsp salt, 5ml/1 tsp sugar and 30ml/2 tbsp oil.

CURRIED PRAWNS IN COCONUT MILK

A curry-like dish where the prawns are cooked in a wonderful spicy coconut gravy.

INGREDIENTS
600ml/1 pint/2½ cups coconut milk
30ml/2 tbsp yellow curry paste
(see Cook's Tip)
15ml/1 tbsp fish sauce
2.5ml/½ tsp salt
5ml/1 tsp granulated sugar
450g/1lb king prawns, shelled, tails left
intact and deveined
225g/8oz cherry tomatoes
juice of ½ lime, to serve
2 red chillies, cut into strips, and
coriander leaves, to garnish

SERVES 4–6

1 Put half the coconut milk into a pan or wok and bring to the boil.

2 Add the yellow curry paste to the coconut milk, stir until it disperses, then simmer for about 10 minutes.

3 Add the fish sauce, salt, sugar and remaining coconut milk. Simmer for another 5 minutes.

4 Add the prawns and cherry tomatoes. Simmer gently for about 5 minutes until the prawns are pink and tender.

5 Serve sprinkled with lime juice and garnished with chillies and coriander.

COOK'S TIP
To make yellow curry paste, process together 6–8 yellow chillies, 1 chopped lemon grass stalk, 4 peeled shallots, 4 garlic cloves, 15ml/1 tbsp peeled chopped root ginger, 5ml/1 tsp coriander seeds, 5ml/1 tsp mustard powder, 5ml/1 tsp salt, 2.5ml/½ tsp ground cinnamon, 15ml/1 tbsp light brown sugar and 30ml/2 tbsp oil in a food processor. When a paste has formed, transfer to a glass jar and chill.

BEAN CURD AND GREEN BEAN RED CURRY

This is another curry that is simple and quick to make. This recipe uses green beans, but you can use almost any kind of vegetable, such as aubergines, bamboo shoots or broccoli.

INGREDIENTS
600ml/1 pint/2½ cups coconut milk
15ml/1 tbsp red curry paste
45ml/3 tbsp fish sauce
10ml/2 tsp palm sugar
225g/8oz button mushrooms
115g/4oz green beans, trimmed
175g/6oz bean curd, rinsed and cut into
2cm/¾in cubes
4 kaffir lime leaves, torn
2 red chillies, sliced
coriander leaves, to garnish

SERVES 4–6

1 Put about one-third of the coconut milk in a wok or saucepan. Cook until it starts to separate and an oily sheen appears.

2 Add the red curry paste, fish sauce and sugar to the coconut milk. Mix together.

3 Add the mushrooms to the curry sauce. Stir and cook for 1 minute.

4 Stir in the rest of the coconut milk and bring back to the boil.

5 Add the green beans and bean curd and simmer gently for another 4–5 minutes.

6 Stir in the torn kaffir lime leaves and sliced chillies. Serve garnished with the coriander leaves.

GREEN BEEF CURRY WITH THAI AUBERGINE

his is a very quick curry to make, so be sure to use tender, good-quality meat.

INGREDIENTS
45ml/3 tbsp vegetable oil
600ml/1 pint/2½ cups coconut milk
450g/1lb beef sirloin
4 kaffir lime leaves, torn
15–30ml/1–2 tbsp fish sauce
5ml/1 tsp palm sugar
150g/5oz small Thai aubergines, halved
a small handful of Thai basil
2 green chillies, shredded to garnish

FOR THE GREEN CURRY PASTE
15 hot green chillies
2 lemon grass stalks, chopped
3 shallots, sliced
2 garlic cloves
15ml/1 tbsp chopped galangal
4 kaffir lime leaves, chopped
2.5ml/½ tsp grated kaffir lime rind
5ml/1 tsp chopped coriander root
6 black peppercorns
5ml/1 tsp coriander seeds, roasted
5ml/1 tsp cumin seeds, roasted
15ml/1 tbsp sugar
5ml/1 tsp salt
5ml/1 tsp shrimp paste (optional)

SERVES 4–6

1 Make the green curry paste. Combine all the ingredients together thoroughly. Pound them in a pestle and mortar or process in a food processor until smooth. Add 30ml/2 tbsp of the oil, a little at a time, and blend well between each addition. Keep in a glass jar in the fridge until required.

2 Heat the remaining oil in a large saucepan or wok. Add 45ml/3 tbsp green curry paste and fry until fragrant.

3 Stir in half the coconut milk, a little at a time. Cook for about 5–6 minutes, until an oily sheen appears.

4 Cut the beef into long thin slices and add to the saucepan with the kaffir lime leaves, fish sauce, sugar and aubergines. Cook for 2–3 minutes, then stir in the remaining coconut milk.

5 Bring back to a simmer and cook until the meat and aubergines are tender. Stir in the Thai basil just before serving. Garnish with the shredded green chillies.

FRIED JASMINE RICE

Thai basil (*bai grapao*), also known as holy basil, has a unique, pungent flavour that is both spicy and sharp. It can be found in most Oriental food markets.

INGREDIENTS
45ml/3 tbsp vegetable oil
1 egg, beaten
1 onion, chopped
15ml/1 tbsp chopped garlic
15ml/1 tbsp shrimp paste
1kg/2¼lb/4 cups cooked jasmine rice
350g/12oz cooked shelled prawns
50g/2oz thawed frozen peas
oyster sauce, to taste
2 spring onions, chopped
15–20 Thai basil leaves, roughly snipped,
plus an extra sprig, to garnish

SERVES 4–6

1 Heat 15ml/1 tbsp of the oil in a wok or frying pan. Add the beaten egg and swirl it around the pan to set like a thin pancake.

2 Cook the egg until golden in colour, slide out on to a board, roll up and cut into thin strips. Set aside.

3 Heat the remaining oil in the wok or large frying pan, add the onion and garlic and fry for 2–3 minutes. Stir in the shrimp paste and mix well.

4 Add the rice, prawns and peas and toss and stir together, until everything is heated through.

5 Season with oyster sauce to taste, taking great care as the shrimp paste is salty. Add the spring onions and basil leaves. Serve topped with the strips of egg pancake. Garnish with a sprig of basil.

FRIED RICE
WITH PORK

If liked, garnish with strips of egg omelette, as in the recipe for Fried Jasmine Rice.

INGREDIENTS
45ml/3 tbsp vegetable oil
1 onion, chopped
15ml/1 tbsp chopped garlic
115g/4oz pork, cut into small cubes
2 eggs, beaten
1kg/2¼lb/4 cups cooked rice
30ml/2 tbsp fish sauce
15ml/1 tbsp dark soy sauce
2.5 ml/½ tsp caster sugar
4 spring onions, finely sliced, 2 red chillies, sliced, 1 lime, cut into wedges, and egg omelette (optional), to garnish

SERVES 4–6

1 Heat the oil in a wok or large frying pan. Add the onion and garlic and cook for about 2 minutes until softened.

2 Add the pork to the softened onion and garlic. Stir-fry until the pork changes colour and is cooked.

3 Add the eggs and cook until scrambled into small lumps.

4 Add the rice and continue to stir and toss, to coat it with the oil and prevent it from sticking.

5 Add the fish sauce, soy sauce and sugar, and mix well. Continue to fry until the rice is thoroughly heated. Garnish with sliced spring onions, red chillies and lime wedges. Top with a few strips of egg omelette, if you like.

SPECIAL CHOW MEIN

L ap cheong is a special air-dried Chinese sausage. It is available from most Chinese supermarkets. If you cannot buy it, substitute for diced ham, chorizo or salami.

INGREDIENTS
45ml/3 tbsp vegetable oil
2 garlic cloves, sliced
5ml/1 tsp chopped root ginger
2 red chillies, chopped
2 lap cheong, about 75g/3oz, rinsed and sliced (optional)
1 boneless chicken breast, thinly sliced
16 uncooked tiger prawns, shelled, tails left intact and deveined
115g/4oz green beans
225g/8oz beansprouts
50g/2oz garlic chives
450g/1lb egg noodles, cooked in boiling water until tender
30ml/2 tbsp soy sauce
15ml/1 tbsp oyster sauce
15ml/1 tbsp sesame oil
salt and freshly ground black pepper
2 spring onions, shredded, and 15ml/1 tbsp coriander leaves, to garnish

SERVES 4–6

1 Heat 15ml/1 tbsp of the oil in a wok or large frying pan and fry the garlic, ginger and chillies. Add the lap cheong (or its substitute), chicken, prawns and beans. Stir-fry for about 2 minutes over a high heat or until the chicken and prawns are cooked. Transfer the mixture to a bowl and set aside.

2 Heat the rest of the oil in the same wok. Add the beansprouts and garlic chives. Stir-fry for 1–2 minutes.

3 Add the noodles and toss and stir to mix. Season with soy sauce, oyster sauce, salt and pepper.

4 Return the prawn mixture to the wok. Reheat and mix well with the noodles. Stir in the sesame oil. Serve garnished with spring onions and coriander leaves.

COCONUT RICE

This dish is usually served with a tangy papaya salad to balance the richness of the coconut.

INGREDIENTS

450g/1lb/2 cups jasmine rice
250ml/8fl oz/1 cup water
475ml/16fl oz/2 cups coconut milk
2.5ml/¹⁄₂ tsp salt
30ml/2 tbsp granulated sugar
fresh shredded coconut, to
garnish (optional)

SERVES 4–6

1 Wash the rice in several changes of cold water until it runs clear. Place the water, coconut milk, salt and sugar in a heavy-based saucepan.

2 Add the rice, cover and bring to the boil. Reduce the heat to low and simmer for about 15–20 minutes or until the rice is tender to the bite and cooked through.

3 Turn off the heat and allow the rice to rest in the pan for 5–10 minutes.

4 Fluff up the rice with chopsticks before serving. Garnish, if you wish, with fresh shredded coconut.

PINEAPPLE FRIED RICE

W hen buying a pineapple, look for a sweet-smelling fruit with an even brownish/yellow skin. To test for ripeness, tap the base – a dull sound indicates that the fruit is ripe. The flesh should also give slightly when pressed.

INGREDIENTS
1 pineapple
30ml/2 tbsp vegetable oil
1 small onion, finely chopped
2 green chillies, seeded and chopped
225g/8oz lean pork,
cut into small dice
115g/4oz cooked shelled prawns
675–900g/1½–2 lb/3–4 cups
cold cooked rice
50g/2oz roasted cashew nuts
2 spring onions, chopped
30ml/2 tbsp fish sauce
15ml/1 tbsp soy sauce
2 red chillies and 1 green chilli, sliced,
and 10–12 mint leaves, to garnish

SERVES 4–6

1 Cut the pineapple in half lengthways and remove the flesh from both halves by cutting round inside the skin. Reserve the skin shells. You need 115g/4oz of fruit, chopped finely (keep the rest for a dessert).

COOK'S TIP
This dish is ideal to prepare for a special-occasion meal. Served in the pineapple skin shells, it is sure to be the talking point of the dinner.

2 Heat the oil in a wok or large frying pan. Add the onion and chillies and fry for about 3–5 minutes until softened. Add the pork and cook until it is brown on all sides.

3 Stir in the prawns and rice and toss well together. Continue to stir-fry until the rice is thoroughly heated. Add the chopped pineapple, cashew nuts and spring onions. Season with fish sauce and soy sauce.

4 Spoon into the pineapple skin shells. Garnish with red and green chillies and shredded mint leaves.

THAI FRIED NOODLES

Phat Thai has a fascinating flavour and texture. It is made with rice noodles and is considered one of the national dishes of Thailand.

INGREDIENTS

350g/12oz rice noodles
45ml/3 tbsp vegetable oil
15ml/1 tbsp chopped garlic
16 uncooked king prawns, shelled, tails
left intact and deveined
2 eggs, lightly beaten
15ml/1 tbsp dried shrimps, rinsed
30ml/2 tbsp pickled white radish
50g/2oz fried bean curd, cut into
small slivers
2.5ml/½ tsp dried chilli flakes
115g/4oz garlic chives,
cut into 5cm/2in lengths
225g/8oz beansprouts
50g/2oz roasted peanuts, coarsely ground
5ml/1 tsp granulated sugar
15ml/1 tbsp dark soy sauce
30ml/2 tbsp fish sauce
30ml/2 tbsp tamarind juice
30ml/2 tbsp coriander leaves and 1 kaffir
lime cut into wedges, to garnish

SERVES 4–6

1 Soak the noodles in warm water for 20–30 minutes, then drain.

2 Heat 15ml/1 tbsp of the oil in a wok or large frying pan. Add the garlic and fry until golden. Stir in the prawns and cook for about 1–2 minutes until pink, tossing from time to time. Remove and set aside.

3 Heat another 15ml/1 tbsp of oil in the wok. Add the eggs and tilt the wok to spread them into a thin sheet. Stir to scramble and break the egg into small pieces. Remove from the wok and set aside with the prawns.

4 Heat the remaining oil in the same wok. Add the dried shrimps, pickled white radish, fried bean curd and dried chilli flakes. Stir briefly. Add the soaked noodles and stir-fry for 5 minutes.

5 Add the garlic chives, half the beansprouts and half the ground peanuts. Season with the granulated sugar, soy sauce, fish sauce and tamarind juice. Mix well and cook until the noodles are heated through.

6 Return the prawn and egg mixture to the wok and mix with the noodles. Serve garnished with the rest of the beansprouts, peanuts, coriander leaves and lime wedges.

TAPIOCA PUDDING

This pudding, made from large, pearl tapioca and coconut milk and served warm, is much lighter than the western-style version. You can adjust the sweetness to your taste. Serve with lychees or the smaller, similar-tasting logans – also known as "dragon's eyes".

INGREDIENTS
115g/4oz tapioca
475ml/16fl oz/2 cups water
175g/6oz granulated sugar
pinch of salt
250ml/8fl oz/1 cup coconut milk
250g/9oz prepared tropical fruits
finely shredded rind of 1 lime,
to decorate

SERVES 4

1 Soak the tapioca in warm water for 1 hour so the grains swell. Drain.

2 Put the water in a saucepan and bring to the boil. Stir in the sugar and salt.

3 Add the tapioca and coconut milk and simmer for about 10 minutes.

4 Serve warm with tropical fruits and decorate with strips of lime rind.

FRIED BANANAS

These delicious treats are a favourite among children and adults alike. They are sold as snacks throughout the day and night at portable roadside stalls and market places. Other fruits such as pineapple and apple work just as well.

INGREDIENTS
115g/4oz plain flour
2.5ml/½ tsp bicarbonate of soda
pinch of salt
30ml/2 tbsp granulated sugar
1 egg
90ml/6 tbsp water
30ml/2 tbsp shredded coconut,
or 15ml/1 tbsp sesame seeds
4 firm bananas
oil, for deep frying
lychees and sprigs of mint, to decorate
30ml/2 tbsp honey, to serve (optional)

SERVES 4

1 Sift the flour, bicarbonate of soda and salt into a bowl. Stir in the granulated sugar. Whisk in the egg and add enough water to make quite a thin batter.

2 Whisk in the shredded coconut or sesame seeds.

3 Peel the bananas. Carefully cut each one in half lengthways, and then crossways.

4 Heat the oil in a wok or deep frying pan. Dip the bananas in the batter, then deep-fry in batches in the oil until golden.

5 Remove from the oil and drain on kitchen paper. Decorate with lychees and sprigs of mint, and serve immediately with honey, if using.

STEWED PUMPKIN IN COCONUT CREAM

Stewed fruit is a popular dessert in Thailand. Use the firm-textured Japanese kabocha pumpkin for this dish, if you can. Bananas and melons can also be prepared in this way, or even sweet-corn kernels or pulses such as mung beans and black beans, in coconut milk.

INGREDIENTS
1kg/2¼lb kabocha pumpkin
750ml/1¼ pint/3 cups coconut milk
175g/6oz granulated sugar
pinch of salt
pumpkin seed kernels, toasted, and
mint sprigs, to decorate

SERVES 4–6

COOK'S TIP
Any pumpkin can be used for this dish, as long as it has a firm texture. Jamaican or New Zealand varieties both make good alternatives to kabocha pumpkin.

1 Wash the pumpkin skin and cut off most of it. Scoop out the seeds.

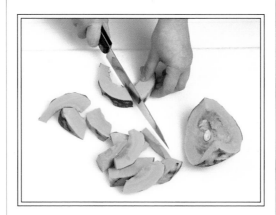

2 Using a sharp knife, cut the flesh into pieces about 5cm/2in in length and 2cm/¾in in thickness.

3 In a saucepan, bring the coconut milk, sugar and salt to the boil.

4 Add the pumpkin and simmer for about 10–15 minutes until the pumpkin is tender. Serve warm. Decorate each serving with a few toasted pumpkin seed kernels and a mint sprig.

BAKED RICE PUDDING, THAI-STYLE

Black glutinous rice, also known as black sticky rice, has long black grains and a nutty taste similar to wild rice. This baked pudding has a distinct character and flavour all of its own.

INGREDIENTS
175g/6oz white or black glutinous (sticky) rice
30ml/2 tbsp soft light brown sugar
475ml/16fl oz/2 cups coconut milk
250ml/8fl oz/1 cup water
3 eggs
30ml/2 tbsp granulated sugar
icing sugar, to decorate

SERVES 4–6

1 Combine the glutinous rice, brown sugar, half the coconut milk and all the water in a saucepan.

2 Bring to the boil and simmer for about 15–20 minutes or until the rice has absorbed most of the liquid, stirring from time to time. Preheat the oven to 150°C/300°F/Gas 2.

3 Transfer the rice into one large ovenproof dish or divide it between individual ramekins. Mix together the eggs, remaining coconut milk and sugar in a bowl.

4 Strain the mixture and pour evenly over the par-cooked rice.

5 Place the dish in a baking tin. Pour in enough boiling water to come halfway up the sides of the dish.

6 Cover the dish with a piece of foil and bake in the oven for about 35 minutes to 1 hour or until the custard is set. Serve warm or cold, sprinkled with icing sugar.

MANGO WITH STICKY RICE

Everyone's favourite dessert. Mangoes, with their delicate fragrance, sweet and sour flavour and velvety flesh, blend especially well with coconut glutinous rice. You need to start preparing this dish the day before.

INGREDIENTS
115g/4oz white glutinous (sticky) rice
175ml/6fl oz/¾ cup thick coconut milk
45ml/3 tbsp granulated sugar
pinch of salt
2 ripe mangoes
strips of lime rind, to decorate

SERVES 4

1 Rinse the glutinous rice thoroughly in several changes of cold water, until the water is clear, then leave to soak overnight in a bowl of fresh, cold water.

2 Drain the rice and spread in an even layer in a steamer lined with some cheesecloth. Cover and steam for about 20 minutes, or until the grains of rice are tender and succulent.

3 Meanwhile, reserve 45ml/3 tbsp of the top of the coconut milk and combine the rest with the sugar and salt in a saucepan. Bring to the boil, stirring until the sugar dissolves, then pour into a bowl and leave to cool a little.

4 Turn the rice into a bowl and pour over the coconut mixture. Stir, then leave for about 10–15 minutes.

5 Peel the mangoes and cut the flesh into slices. Place on top of the rice and drizzle over the reserved coconut milk. Decorate with strips of lime rind.

COCONUT CUSTARD

This traditional dish can be baked or steamed and is often served with sweet glutinous rice and a selection of fruits such as mango and persimmon.

INGREDIENTS
4 eggs
75g/3oz soft light brown sugar
250ml/8fl oz/1 cup coconut milk
5ml/1 tsp vanilla, rose or
jasmine extract
mint leaves and icing sugar, to decorate

SERVES 4–6

COOK'S TIP
Coconut milk can be obtained directly from coconut flesh – this gives the creamiest milk. It is also available in a can, as a soluble powder and in block form. Coconut milk which is pre-packaged in this way makes a useful addition to sauces and dressings.

1 Preheat the oven to 150°C/300°F/ Gas 2. Whisk the eggs and sugar in a bowl until smooth. Add the coconut milk and vanilla or other extract and blend well.

2 Strain the mixture and pour into individual ramekins or a cake tin.

3 Stand the ramekins or tin in a roasting pan. Carefully fill the pan with hot water to reach halfway up the outsides of the ramekins or tin.

4 Bake for about 35–40 minutes or until the custards are set. Test with a fine skewer or cocktail stick.

5 Remove from the oven and leave to cool. Turn out and serve with sliced fruit. Decorate with mint leaves and icing sugar.

INDEX